Break Free by Changing Your Inner Story

BROOKE KREBILL

Copyright ©2021 by Brooke Krebill

All rights reserved. No part of this book may be reproduced or used in any manner without written permission of the copyright owner except for the use of quotations in a book review.

VISIT **BROOKEKREBILL.COM** TO DOWNLOAD YOUR FREE WORKBOOK, WHICH INCLUDES THE EXERCISES FOR EACH CHAPTER, ALONG WITH STAYING UP TO DATE ON EVENTS AND ANNOUNCEMENTS.

CONTENTS

INTRODUCTION   11

CHAPTER 1 *Mock - Elections*   19

CHAPTER 2 *The College Days*   27

CHAPTER 3. *Unconditional Love*   35

CHAPTER 4. *Waking Up*   47

CHAPTER 5. *The Lies Must Be Destroyed*   55

CHAPTER 6. *Mom*   63

CHAPTER 7. *Relationships*   75

CHAPTER 8. *Boundaries*   83

CHAPTER 9. *Therapy*   93

CHAPTER 10. *Own Your Story.*   101

CHAPTER 11. *What Do You Desire?*   111

ABOUT THE AUTHOR   121

DEDICATIONS

To my amazing children, Benjamin and Isabel, you are both my greatest joy and my proudest accomplishment.

INTRODUCTION

Welcome! My wish is that there is something in here that helps you begin to find your best self and live out your purpose. I come to you with full transparency, owning my faults, taking responsibly for where my life was before, where my life is now, and where it is now headed. You'll find in this book that I didn't have a rough upbringing. You'll likely read my stories and wonder what in the hell was wrong with me and why I made some of the decisions I'm sharing with you. My hope is that you realize that no matter our backgrounds, we hold the power within us to change and become whomever we desire. You'll see that I have self-sabotaged, caused myself unnecessary pain, and spoke to myself in a manner that I wouldn't speak to my own worst enemy.

Growing up, I felt different than other people. I felt I had no place in school, I was a daydreamer at its finest, and although I had friends, I struggled with having close connections. At the age of 12, these feelings were defined to me as being an airhead, and the inner story began that I was stupid. I lived this lie for many, many years. Throughout this book, you will see how that replay of being stupid impacted almost every decision I made in my teens and twenties.

We all have defining moments in our lives. Just like you, I have several. For many, many years, I felt as if no one understood me. Others would give me advice or talk about how great their own lives were, and although I smiled and pretended to be interested, inside I'd think to myself, "Yep, they just don't get it. They will never understand my situation." For way too long, I allowed myself to be a victim, thought my story was unique, and relied on others for my own happiness. I didn't realize that becoming the person I desired to be began with my relationship with myself. I didn't know that I could truly celebrate others when I became confident in who I was.

I'll walk you through what I told myself as a single mom of two beautiful children. I'll also walk you through my journey of relationships; how I created healthy boundaries; dealt with the sudden death of my mother via car accident; and how my inner voice began to change, which impacted my relationships, my business, and my outlook on life.

I relied on others for my happiness and when they failed to hit my expectations, I became angry, depressed and alone. You'll find in my stories that this did me no good. You'll see how I came to love myself, own my story, forgive others (most importantly, myself) and become confident in who I am. My hope is that by sharing these stories, you may be able to change your inner self talk. You'll find that your outside circumstances, the opinions of others, and the decisions you made in the past have zero control over your future; however, first you must learn to listen to your inner spirit.

Does this mean I still don't struggle with the nagging voice of self-sabotage? No way! It only means that I have learned how to quiet that ugly voice down by telling myself a new story. If you're wondering how I did that, this is the book for you!!

I now know that during the days I felt most in pain, I likely also caused pain for others. I realize now that hurting people hurt people. I also realize that those who are confident and love who they are, are most likely to bring out the best in others. I believe my purpose is to bring out the best in you. When we listen intently to our intuition, we realize that our purpose here on earth is not only to expand and grow, but it's far greater and more powerful than one's own personal fulfillment.

I believe in a higher power, and I believe that higher power is within all of us. The nudges we feel don't come by accident—they come to help us realize our purpose. I now understand that the depression and anxiety I suffered from for many years was because I was in conflict with myself. The constant lies I told myself over and over were not in alignment with my purpose. I didn't know how to listen to my own inner being, nor really understand that I even had one. I chose to listen to how others defined me and created a story inside my head that was negative, ugly, and untrue. The more I listened to this story, the more my life began to look like it.

*Un*CAGED

Why did I name this book "UnCaged?" My astronomy sign is Leo, and although I know very little about astronomy, I can tell you that a lion stuck in a cage is the perfect description of how I felt most of my young life. I would constantly beat myself up for not living up to the standard I set for myself, but I didn't realize how to change that. I'll take you on my journey of not only how I spoke to myself and self-sabotaged, but also the journey of what caused change within me.

After over a decade of having a business coach, working with a personal coach, finding amazing mentors, going through therapy, and learning to look to a higher power for the answers, my life has unfolded in ways that I never knew possible. If you're reading this book, that is the true testament of my inner self-talk having influence over my life. Looking back at old journals of where I began goal setting, I had the goal of being an author, a speaker, and an influencer written down for five years before I did anything about it. My intuition told me for many years that this is what I was meant to do. I felt it in my bones, but I lacked a burning desire to accomplish it. My lack of burning desire simply came from not believing I deserved it. I was full of excuses as to why I'd never be able to accomplish this.

My inner self-talk began to shift after suddenly losing my mom to a car accident. My mom was the outside voice cheering me on and protecting me. After she was taken, I had to learn how to do this for myself. I'll walk you through the journey of how transformation really began by doing this. My wish in writing this book is that you realize your worth, without your world turning upside down first.

The year was 2020 when I began writing the book you're being introduced to now. 2020 was a year of the COVID-19 pandemic, our entire economy was shut down, my industry (Real Estate) was deemed as non-essential for three months in my state, I had staff on my payroll (with no work for them), and I spent more time at home than I knew was even possible. I was a single mom of two teens who are social and had a horrible time dealing with the inability to see others.

2020 was also a year of the most intense presidential election I've witnessed in my lifetime, social media blow-ups over politics, and the world around me living in fear of what the future held. Although I made an educated decision on my own personal vote, I chose not to become emotionally involved, as I finally had the strength and the knowledge to know that my future depended solely on my own thoughts, actions, and determination. Understand that I am not naïve enough to think that our environment doesn't make an impact, but the real power comes from within. I knew that what I became emotionally involved in and expected was precisely what my future would hold; therefore, I chose what to become emotionally involved in.

Throughout the pandemic and the presidential election, I was crazy enough to keep the news off. The death counts from COVID-19 were beginning to make me feel extremely depressed, the shutdown of the economy was making me panic, the election was making me feel anxiety, and I was afraid to say anything in fear of upsetting someone. My strength, my voice, and everything I knew to be true was being highly tested. Therefore, I chose to turn off the news, concentrate on what I had control over, and shift to become emotionally involved in finding things that brought me joy. While the majority of the world kept the news on, I chose meditation and prayer. I became closer to those I love through Zoom, and I wrote a damn book! This, my friends, is how telling myself a new story, not allowing outside circumstances to have control over me, and getting in tune with my inner spirit has changed how I live.

Our lives are a direct reflection of the questions we ask ourselves, how we ask them, what answers we expect, and being open to listening to our intuition when the answer arrives. Ask a victim question and you'll get a victim answer. Throughout this book, you'll find examples of victim mindset questions that keep us caged, and you'll find examples of questions that will break you free! I'll challenge you to be your best self, I'll make you uncomfortable, and I'll be your biggest cheerleader along the way!

You'll find I write like I talk, I am no English expert, and I'm direct in how I speak. If you can hang with that, read on and get ready, wake up your own lioness, and let her roar!

CHAPTER 1 *Mock - Elections*

The labels we choose to believe are the labels we allow to define us.

The year was 1990. I was 12 years old, a nervous wreck, and hoping to appear calm and cool on my first day of seventh grade. I was entering a new school and I wanted to be perfect. I left my old private school for, what seemed to me, a huge public middle school. On the inside, I was terrified and excited, all at the same time. On the outside, I was hoping to appear calm, cool, and collected.

My bangs were stiff and standing high, just the way I liked them, and my jeans were tight rolled beautifully. I was feeling fine. As I walked in, I quickly noticed all the students and decided right away whom I'd approach and attempt to make friends with.

It seems crazy to think that we pick our friends based on how they look and how they handle themselves. But this doesn't happen only in middle school. Let's face it; sadly, most of us do this in our adult lives too. We quickly learn that we are most comfortable when we surround ourselves with those who appear to be like us or who we desire to be. (You will get more on that "comfort zone" throughout this book. Hang tight, my friend.)

The year went well, for the most part. I made friends, and I seemed to be liked by most people. However, my grades were awful, and I quickly learned that studying wasn't quite my thing. At my new school, we were given progress reports and were expected to show our parents. They then were expected to sign the report, and the student was to return the signed report back to school. It was nothing like in my old private school. Nope, at that school, they made a phone call home if something seemed off. You'd then have the privilege to stay after class and get extra schooling along with being asked to move your desk right next to the teachers. Aha, yes, making sure that you stayed focused—I know this firsthand.

This new school was freedom, no call home. No need to stay after school, all I had to do was get that progress report signed. Not a problem. Wait, except for I was a solid C student, likely with a D+ sprinkled in there every now and then. Nope. No way. That all-too-familiar fear set in. I was not showing my parents this, so I did what any responsible student would do. I took it upon myself to sign my mom's name. Boom. Easy peasy. I turned it in. And I was done.

However, there was also this thing called parent-teacher conferences, and my parents dared to go. So, it began; they found out I forged my mom's signature and that my grades were in the pits. Let's say that it was not a fun evening for me after they arrived home.

From this day forward, I dreaded parent-teacher conferences. It became the norm that I'd get called upstairs when my three siblings were asked to stay downstairs and watch TV.

I got the same "Why aren't you trying?" and "If you just spend as much time on your schoolwork as you do your hair" chat. Oh, the fun times.

I'd also like to point out that my sister, who is just 18 months younger than me, was a stellar student. I swear she even wanted to study (okay, let's be honest here—she's ridiculously gifted and likely didn't need to study much, if at all). She loved report card and parent-teacher conference days; she made sure my parents would never forget these special days of hers.

Don't get me wrong, I love my sister dearly. Today we are the best of friends. But on report card days, not so much.

In the eighth grade, I was introduced to mock-elections. Wow. I had never known such a thing. Now, if you're not familiar with what those are, allow me to engage you. The students actually vote on which of the students is best suited for categories such as class clown, best dresser, biggest flirt, most likely to succeed, etc.

Oh, how I wanted to be voted for something. I mean, come on, if you get voted for something, anything, that is way better than being well, than being invisible! The nerves of being the new girl in school set in, and I wondered if I was known well enough to be on the ballot.

And so, I'm the lucky one that was voted class airhead. Yep. Class airhead. Yay me, I was known for something. Yes, I found out that I was known by my peers as being the dumb one for the first time. The ditzy one. The airhead.

Although I was embarrassed by this, even at the age of 12, I must have unconsciously thought to myself, "I shall be just that." And so my peers once again awarded me the same mock election in my senior year of high school—class airhead.

This time it didn't quite have the same effect. This time it stung, and it stung hard. I was upset. I was more than upset; I was horribly embarrassed, hurt, and sad. It was a label I didn't want. And I sure as heck didn't want my picture in the yearbook with this label next to me. Too bad it was there, it is there, it is forever my identity. I mean, come on, it's in the high school yearbook.

I get it. Lighten up! I know. I hear you. But at the time, I didn't realize that I had allowed this to have the effect on me that it did.

Our words matter. Our actions matter. How we label people matters. And my gosh, I pray and I hope I was kind to others. I pray that others don't think of me as the one who said ugly, unkind words that had long-term effects on them. Unfortunately, I fear I did. Of course I did. Misery loves company, and those who are hurting (and hiding it) are likely going to hurt others.

I get that this is how kids act. I am not oblivious, but we must do better! I cannot imagine what would have happened during that time if there were social media in the mix. There was no Internet or computer when I was in school. Oh, and cell phones? Ha! There was no such thing. I laugh and tell my kids that we had to call the house phone and get the parents' permission to chat with their child, back in my day. What a different world we live in now.

I can assure you that people can say uglier things when sitting behind a computer than they will in person, and this has got to stop!

For nearly 30 years I told myself that I was an airhead. For nearly 30 years I allowed a reputation, that I so firmly believed, to define me as an adult. I continually repeated to myself that I wasn't brilliant, that I was seen as an airhead, and that good grades weren't in the books for me.

Because this inner dialogue was so ingrained in me, I proved this right with every action I took, and unknowingly. I was making decisions based on what I thought about myself. The inner dialogue was very much like, "Sure, go to college, you'll drop out anyway." "You better stay cute because you'll never be anything else." "I'm the dumb one of the family." "Party away, girl! It's better to be fun than to fail at anything worthwhile."

And that's precisely how my life looked for many years. I went to college. I came back home. I tried college again, came home, took time off, went to a community college, and never had any direction.

In fact, I had such little direction that I couldn't stand the thought of being with myself and my thoughts, so I partied. My self-esteem was in the pits and I was paralyzed with anxiety and fear.

When we tell ourselves one thing, our minds will find reasons to prove what we tell ourselves is right; there really is no other way. What we expect must happen. I expected to be treated as an airhead, I expected to get bad grades, and I expected to fail. So that's precisely what I (unconsciously) looked for.

When we expect a particular result, we must prove ourselves right. Otherwise, we'd feel crazy. Some people call it the law of attraction—others call it the universe, energy, source, or God. If you ask for it, it will arrive. Perhaps not in your perfect timing, but when you are ready for it. What we focus on shows up! It does not matter if we want it or not. What matters is what we choose to get emotionally engaged in and focus on. I was emotionally focused on the idea that I was dumb. I didn't realize that the power to change was always within me.

I believe that we have an inner being, a spirit, a soul, and I think that our actions are not in line with our inner being when we feel conflict. Our inner spirit will never steer us in the wrong direction. The younger me was not in touch with my inner being.

Unless we are in touch with our inner being, we will listen to what other people and our environment tell us we are. I would talk to myself in a manner that I would not speak to my worst enemy.

So, with that said, I could never visualize myself graduating or in a career that would ever be worth talking about. I had no direction. I was lost. I had no goals. I didn't know what I wanted. I didn't know who I was.

One day after waiting tables, it dawned on me that I should probably go to college. My siblings were all there, I was 21, I had an apartment with a roommate who barely spoke to me, and I wasn't just living paycheck to paycheck; I was living day to day.

Back when I waited tables, if I needed money, I'd go to the restaurant during the shift change and beg others to give up their shift. Poof—there you have it (most of the time). But I was tired, and I was sick of my feet hurting. I was sick of being broke, and if I'm being honest with myself, I was jealous of my siblings who were all at college making memories, and I was afraid of missing out on them. I also knew that no one would do this for me. It was going to be up to me. And if I didn't do something, my life would look like this forever.

CHAPTER 2 *The College Days*

We rise (and fall) to the level of which others expect of us!

I did not know that I was sabotaging myself by how I was speaking to myself. I made a decision. I went to college again but had no direction. I was in college, but my self-talk remained ugly. I went into business and decided to pursue a marketing degree without even knowing what marketing was. In my head, it was sales, and that was about it. My older brother had a marketing degree, my younger brother was there pursuing the same, and I figured, "Okay, that sounds good." I can do something with that. I can convince anyone of anything, or so I thought. That's right, I have the exact same degree, from the exact same college, as my two brothers. I can hear you asking about my sister right now. No worries, she was a marketing major as

27

well, although hers would be nothing short of a master's degree. Okay fine, I may have been a wee bit jealous of her growing up.

It was a lucky day when I walked into my Marketing 101 class. My professor saw something in me. This is the first time I genuinely felt seen by a teacher as a gift and not a challenge. And he wasn't afraid to say it. He wasn't afraid to tell the class that he thought that I was gifted in this area. I look at that day, and I remember how I felt. It was a big class, and I don't know what I said, but I raised my hand to participate. He stopped the class, asked me to repeat what I said, and publicly propelled me for my answer.

Isn't it amazing how one person can drastically affect our lives, and they usually don't even know it? I did graduate, and my marketing professor was there. He made it a point to be the one to hand me my diploma.

It was that moment where I decided, yep, this was going to for sure be my degree. It was actually that first day that I remember thinking, "I'm going to do this. I am going to graduate from college."

Now, allow me to say something. I came from an environment that encouraged education. The only person holding me back was me. I also want to say that I realize how lucky I am because of this. I don't have a horrible sob story of childhood; I'm one of four kids. We did the regular sibling fights and two minutes later we would be best friends. With two boys and two girls, and with the oldest and the youngest only six years apart, we knew how to fight and how to get along from birth. We had to share rooms, in many cases we shared the same friends, and although my siblings were my first friends, we easily got on each other's nerves as well.

My parents were loving. I have memories of laughing and fighting. I have memories of family dinners. My upbringing was a good one. And I want to reiterate that I know how lucky I am because of this. I've been really blessed. It wasn't them that held me back. It was me.

Allow me to say there were areas of my life that I was confident in. I was a cheerleader. And I loved cheerleading. I can hear you now ... This may be why you had an airhead reputation—pffft, yeah yeah.

I still look at my cheerleading days with nothing but fond memories. You do have to have talent, and you have to be athletic—that's right, I am defending this great sport of mine. I was loud. I was proud. I had school spirit. I liked being front and center at the football games. I was really pleased to be the captain of that cheerleading squad, and some of my best friends were on that squad with me. But school? That was not something I was confident in. I kept my high school GPA just high enough to be able to participate in cheerleading.

Because I had a professor who saw more in me than I was able to see at the time, I got through the college years too. I realize college is not for everyone. I don't even need a degree to do what I do for a living, but for me, it's exactly what I needed at that particular time. I needed to realize that I could accomplish something, anything. As a potential graduate, I had to realize that a 10-hour workday of waiting tables was more painful than studying and staying complacent (which is exactly what my fear of failure was doing to me).

This is what we must do with everything—get uncomfortable and take the chance. We have to make the conscious decision to change and know that we are worthy of our desires. We must see it in our minds before it actually comes to fruition. What we think about most is actually what happens to our lives. This was the first time I had ever visualized myself achieving, what was to me, such an accomplishment.

The story before that, though, was that I was dumb. I told myself that I was an airhead. And you know what? This was an excellent excuse not to have to work hard because, well, I'd fail anyway. That story I told myself was a lie. The story I told myself was an exact reflection of what my self-image was at the time. I talked to myself in a horrible manner. My self-esteem was low. I cared way too much about what other people thought of me and way too little about what I thought of myself.

Here's the real story. The real story is that not one person in my family or my *close* friends thought I was incapable, dumb, or an airhead. My parents encouraged me the entire way. And the entire way, they cringed as I self-sabotaged and allowed my inner voice to be nasty. I was always capable of getting an education, and they never told me differently.

Sometimes we don't hear what those who are close to us are saying. This may be due to our inner voice saying, "Yeah, yeah... you love me, you're supposed to say that." When a perfect stranger sees the same thing that those who love you see, believe them. Believe all of them—those who love you, and those who see greatness in you. Your

Creator sees greatness in you, and your inner spirit wants nothing more than for you to see it too.

This is important for me to say—I do not believe the only acceptable education is a college one. Oh no, my friends, knowledge comes in all forms. Later in life, I learned that I was not dumb at all. I just happened to learn differently than your typical student. I wasn't your average kid who could sit in a room all day and concentrate. I'm a dreamer, a risk-taker, a doer, and I'm an all-over-the-place type of thinker.

At this very moment, your life is an exact reflection of the thoughts you had in the past. Read that again! The thoughts from the past. If you want to change your future, you must first change your thoughts today.

The thought still creeps in me that I'm the class airhead. But today, that thought comes less frequently. I still question myself. I sometimes still wonder if I'm good enough to do that or if I am good enough to do this. I know I can't control all of my thoughts, but I also know that I manage which thoughts I become emotionally involved in. This is key! The thoughts we become emotionally involved in are the loudest thoughts. Choose wisely.

Here is my warning—I am not the friend that tells you what I think you want to hear! I am the kind of friend who speaks the truth as I see it. No hurt feelings are allowed here. K? K!

First thing first. Can we agree that we are now adults? You are not responsible for what happened to you as a child. You are not responsible for how you ever felt as a child or how you interpreted your world. This is not your fault! BUT, and here is the big but ... You are absolutely responsible for doing something about it. We get to a certain point in life where excuses don't work! They don't change your life. They are just that, excuses! Easy? Nope! Worth the hard work? I suppose that's up to you! Do you want to be a victim, or do you want to change? You cannot have both.

Not only did I graduate from college, I also had every reason to quit my senior year. That's right. I became pregnant during my senior year of college, my son attended my graduation ceremony at the age of one, and that's where the new story begins.

Victim or Victor?

Victim mindset questions begin with "why." When we ask a victim question, we get a victim answer. For example, "Why does this person treat me this way?" Answer - "Because you are a bother." Or "Why am I unable to do this?" Answer - "Because you are incapable." A victim question will give you an excuse as your answer.

Victor questions begin with "how" or "what." Ask a victor question, get the answer that sets you free.

The question that keeps the lioness tame—"Why am I such an airhead and why I can't I concentrate like everyone else?"

The question that sets her free— "What differences do I have that can be utilized as my strengths?"

ACTION STEPS

Affirmations: Don't tell me it's hokey or that it doesn't work unless you've done it for 30 days consistently!

1. Take a look at your life and think of it as a mirror of your thoughts. Results don't lie. What areas have room for opportunity?

2. Write down the thought that gave you those results. "I feel like I'm an idiot, so my result is I fail to achieve the goals I set for myself."

3. Then write the exact opposite of that thought. For example, "I feel (insert emotion) now that I have achieved (insert goal)!" "I (feel energized, excited, and accomplished) now that I have achieved (the sales goal of hitting 25 million)." Remember, this is your GOAL. Write it down in the present tense, as if it's already happened.

4. Tear up, burn, or throw away the thoughts written in step #2.

5. Spend 20 minutes a day reading aloud, focusing on, and visualizing the thoughts written in step #3. Do not just read it. Become emotionally involved in it! That is the key.

CHAPTER 3. *Unconditional Love*

If we don't change that inner voice for ourselves, let's at least do it for our littles who are watching.

Shortly after New Year's Day in my senior year of college, I just knew something was off; I didn't feel right. I felt sick and tired. Not just tired, more like exhausted. I had only met my boyfriend's family over the holidays, and things seemed to be going quite well. Until I dropped the bomb on him that I was pregnant. We were young, he was younger, and in no way were we prepared to be parents.

The stress between us was real, and I spent the first part of my pregnancy single (uh-huh), getting most of my nutrition from ice cream, and living mostly alone. Thank God for my brother who spent quite a bit of time at my place checking on me, and of course, helping me indulge in a tub of ice cream.

I gained an impressive 90 pounds throughout the pregnancy. That's what happens when you are depressed, single, have no self-esteem, and find yourself pregnant and alone with your thoughts.

The phone call to my mom was one I will never forget. I was in my apartment, and I knew I had to call her. It had been a few days since we last chatted, and I assumed she was beginning to get suspicious that something was going on. I called her while she was at work to check in, and she immediately said, "What's wrong? I'm going into a different room, and you're going to tell me. You're pregnant, aren't you?"

This woman just knew things, and it drove me nuts. Her intuition was ridiculous. She was always two steps ahead of me; she was probably two steps ahead of all four of us kids. She was a great mom, but I would have preferred her to be just a little less intuitive this time. Yep. I was pregnant, and I was trapped; I had to tell her over the phone while she was at work. Awesome. Her next words, after a long, deep breath, were, "Oh, this is good, this is really good, your party days are over."

I never had to think about what a parent goes through when a child goes to college, or a child like me anyway. She was right. I was a party girl, and college was a little crazy, even for this girl.

My life would never look like I knew it before. I had to think of a child, my child. I was responsible for this child's well-being. I endured a long semester, feeling alone, being pregnant, going to class with a huge belly—who am I kidding?! Fine, I had a colossal, everything! (I looked about nine months pregnant when I was probably four—not kidding.) I was embarrassed. I was ashamed, and I wanted to hide.

The relationship between his father and me was a toxic one. We attract what we believe we are worthy of, which is reflected by our internal thoughts. When our thoughts are not aligned with what our inner spirit knows to be truth, we become in conflict with ourselves. I did not like myself, and at the time, I had no idea why; however, we sure did make beautiful human beings.

We actually did become engaged and pregnant again with our beautiful daughter. That's right—two children out of wedlock. And the relationship was not something that I'd wish for my children to be in the same household as. I knew at that point that I had two choices. One, I could raise these two beautiful children in a home that was not loving and likely could end in divorce, or two, I could leave early on and have them know no different. I chose the latter.

As I always did, I called my mom to explain. She was my rock. Her words were, "Do not go through this alone. Come home. We will help you." And so I did, with a one and a half-year-old and four months pregnant. I ended up back in my own hometown, had to put my tail between my legs (again), live back at home (again), and raise two kids out of wedlock. That did not do a whole lot for the self-esteem.

I look at that moment of life, and I have nothing but respect for the men and women who raise children completely alone. Don't get me wrong, I did the hard work, but my parent's help and love for my kids cannot go unmentioned here. They were my co-parents. And I am beyond grateful for this.

I started a job managing a restaurant soon after my children's father and I broke it off for good, I was five months pregnant with my daughter, and soon after, both kids were in daycare. I'm not sure if you've ever put your kids in daycare or not, but holy shit. It is more expensive than I had ever imagined. The cost for both of them to attend daycare full time was over the average mortgage payment. I am in no way saying they (meaning those who watch our children) are not worth every cent. I am simply saying that I had no idea!

So, we lived with my parents much (much) longer than I had anticipated doing so. I remember calling the state to ask if I could apply for some assistance; I needed help with daycare expenses. The lady on the phone asked me what my income was, and after I told her, she chuckled and said, "Oh honey, for your family of three, you don't qualify for help."

I did not know how I was going to make ends meet. I did not know how I would be able to get out of my parents' home. I did not know how I would be able to provide a life that my children so deserved. I told myself I was stuck; I told myself I was worthless. I felt useless; I felt helpless. I felt like I had no other way. I asked the lady on the phone what I should do, and she literally said, without hesitation, "You'd be better off unemployed and staying home with your kids," and she was not kidding. Now, I understand that not everyone has the option that I had. I realize many parents must stay at home with their

38

kids to make ends meet. I do understand why government assistance is needed.

I also understand that I had several choices, during and after my pregnancies, that you may feel would have been better for me. I was approached with all of them (on several occasions). I made the decision that was right for me. Make no mistake, I honor every woman's personal decision on what to do in this situation. I honor a woman's decision in every way. I don't walk in anyone else's shoes, and nobody else walks in mine. We must stand together and not reprimand each other for the choices we make. We do the best we can with what we know and have at the time. Let's leave the judgment up to the One who knows all, and that is not us.

Because I did have the help and support from my parents, I chose to continue to work and not receive help from the government. I continued to work full time, continued to live with my supportive parents, and continued to keep my children in daycare.

We eventually did get ahead. We moved into a two-bedroom apartment and shortly after rented a house, but it was a financial struggle for me the entire time. I remember being too proud to ask for help when I needed it. I remember being in such a deep hole that I didn't know how I would pay for rent and have to come up with all sorts of excuses. I wasn't a big spender. But I will tell you, I wasn't a really good budgeter either.

I was terribly embarrassed, ashamed, and continued the same cycle of speaking to myself as if I were nothing. Without my parent's help, I'm not confident I would have been able to break through that

39

time. I am eternally grateful to the loving parents I've been blessed with. I give major kudos to those who make it through tough times without the same kind of support.

So here I was, single, broke, overworked, and a mom. I asked myself why in the hell I had worked so hard for a college education if this is how my life was going to end up anyway. Single, broke, and in a two-bedroom apartment that I could barely keep the lights on in.

Again, that's the story I was telling myself. I told myself that this would be my life forever, I'd be broke and alone, and that no one would ever want to be with a woman who had two children out of wedlock. I told myself that I was a sinner and damaged goods and that I'd never make it out (Oh, that Catholic guilt was strong).

If this doesn't resonate, think of someone you know who complains about everything. They complain about how little money they have, how their boss is a jerk, and how their marriage is in the pits. How are they living the next time you speak to them? That's right! The exact same and still complaining about anything that anyone will listen to over and over. Why? I blame this on being fixed-minded. Instead of looking on the inside, fixed-minded people blame everything and everyone else for their issues rather than their very own inner dialogue and beliefs. It's easier to blame everyone else rather than take responsibility and decide to make a change. The ego is a very hard thing to overcome!

Now think of the person who seeks joy and has a positive outlook on life. This person likely speaks highly of their family, finds blessings in all situations (even when things aren't perfect), doesn't engage in gossip, and understands growing, expanding, and creating is what we are here to do. They accept responsibility for their adult decisions, and they don't allow their own egos to keep them complacent. What are their results the next time? That's right. They are still positive and joyful.

What we become emotionally involved in is what we attract. Complaining will bring you more things to complain about. When we find joy, we find more things to find joy in.

The only thing broken about me was that I had broken thoughts. Those broken thoughts kept me stuck. My inner voice was, once again, my worst enemy, and my inner voice kept me embarrassed, ashamed, and broke for way too long. That story was a lie. The negativity I kept inside of me was easier to believe rather than learn how to change it. Keeping this story allowed me to be a victim. The story you're telling yourself right now, yeah, that may be a lie, too. We've got to do better; we've got to do better for ourselves and our kids and society as a whole. We've got to tell ourselves a new story. We're telling ourselves one anyway, so just make up a different one. Make it a better one. Make it a crazy, fantastic one. What you focus on expands, and what you expect is what you will get, so get all the good.

I think about how life would have changed sooner if I had told myself a different story. What would have happened if I knew the power of my thoughts then? What if I told myself that I was a kick-ass mom who chose to get her children out of an unhealthy environment? That I decided to get them into a loving home? That this kick-ass mom had an education, a job, a dream, a brain, and enough determination and love in her heart to teach her children that they are worth beautiful things? That they are worth all of their dreams coming true? What if I had set that example and persevered and told myself that I was, in fact, worth it too? I would have taught them to never let anyone tell them differently. I would have taught them that this kick-ass mom believed it was possible for her as well.

I now know that's the real story, but it took a lot of healing. Well, let me tell you, it took a lot of counseling. It took thousands and thousands of dollars in coaching, which by the way, I didn't always have. It took tragic loss and for my world to be shaken up. Healing and change didn't happen by chance, it happened because of a burning desire to live my life differently. Through personal development, I learned that my life, business, and leadership directly reflect my personal image and personal growth. I had a lot of work to do.

Once again, I got what I expected at that time. I stayed victim for way too long. I expected to be hurt, to fail, and to be damaged. My results were precisely in line with my self-image. Again, as they always are.

I'll never forget the day that my son came home from school and said, "We had to write about our heroes today. I wrote about you."

Woah! If you get nothing else from this book, get this! Your kids think of you as their hero regardless of how you feel about yourself! This child of mine is bright, intelligent, and will change the world he lives in. He is capable and doing amazing things! Although he said this to me at a young age, I knew even then that he was put on Earth to make a difference. If I didn't step up and be the hero he deserved to have, how would he embrace the idea of being brave and going for big things? If he's watching me and looking up to me, I better give him something to look up to!

Today, I look at both of my children and am in awe at how blessed I am. As with any parent, I was madly in love with them from day one. Both of them bring so much joy to my life. They are both talented, hilarious, kind, and deeply special in their own ways. When I look at them, I am grateful for their father. I am grateful for my parents who so generously helped raise them. I am grateful for my ex-husband, who generously and freely still loves them as his own. I am grateful that they saw me struggle to make ends meet, as they now understand the value of hard work. I am grateful that I needed to grow up quickly to be a good mom. And I am forever grateful to be chosen as the one who gets to be called "mom" by them.

Had I concentrated on this, rather than how tough things were or what I was missing out on, I dare say that things would have looked a bit different for us much sooner.

We're here to learn lessons and expand, and if we don't learn those lessons, life has a funny sense of humor. Those lessons will keep on showing up until we do learn them. Make no mistake, what you focus on expands.

*Un*CAGED

Victim or Victor?

The question that keeps the lioness tame— "Why can't I have a life that isn't a constant struggle?"

The question that sets her free— "How do I turn my situation around and provide for my children in the way they deserve?"

ACTION STEPS

Appreciation: Until we are grateful for what we have, we will not be blessed with more. My interpretation of this is that if we are not grateful, focus on the negative, and bitch and moan about what we don't have, the universe, God, and our spirit whisper, "You're not ready for more blessings until you are grateful for what has already been provided."

Do this daily! When you wake up and before you go to bed.

1. Write down all that you are grateful for. If this is not easy for you, begin with the idea of clean air and water, a roof over your head, shoes on your feet, etc. There is always something to be grateful for.

2. Be thoughtful when doing this. FEEL your gratitude! Feeling is key here. If you don't "feel" grateful for something at the time, and it brings up negativity, don't put it on the list that day. You must FEEL gratitude, not negativity.

CHAPTER 4. *Waking Up*

The lioness begins to roar.

Our creator brings people into our lives for a purpose. Sometimes we are the teacher, and sometimes we are the student.

I had a rare night out when my kids were ages three and one, and I met a gentleman who would soon become a "teacher" of mine. We ended up talking for about eight months or so. At the time, I felt extremely broken (I think you know this by now), and this guy liked me. I couldn't believe it.

Although that relationship was nothing to get too excited about, the change in me over those eight months, and the following, are worth speaking about. I'll never forget the first time he showed up at my house with a wrapped gift for me, for no apparent reason, as it wasn't a holiday or my birthday. You can imagine my excitement, well, until I opened it up. It was a book. Yep, a book. I can confidently say that at this time of my life, I had never read a book for pure pleasure. I don't remember what book it was, but it was some sort of self-help book, and I was horribly offended! I felt like he was telling me that I needed to change. I felt like he was trying to say to me that I wasn't good enough. My first reaction was to be upset. If you know me, I don't hide my emotions well. I typically don't need to literally say what I think as my face will tell it for me anyway.

His reaction was calm, and he told me he read it, loved it, that it changed his life, and he wished for me to have the same experience. Not because he felt like I needed it, but because he felt like I deserved it. Reluctantly, I read that book.

I wanted more information. A little background on this hottie: He was part of a direct selling company, and this particular company mainly focused on self-help material. The company sold content such as CDs, books, and meetings. I was hooked. (In case I just aged myself, an audio CD is a round disc that we listened to music and voice on.) I couldn't get enough information on this. This is where I learned that I'm capable of great things and that all of us have greatness within us. The information on this topic was new to me. It was exciting, and I was ready to take on the world.

I've been a dreamer my whole life. I've always felt a little bit like a lion in a cage. I'm a risk-taker. I'm someone that doesn't follow all the rules, but I knew no different. I grew up working-class, with mostly working-class people in our community. We learned to get good grades, go to school, put our boots on, and get to work. Entrepreneurship, dreaming, and getting uncomfortable were not things I was taught. That meant risk. It meant no guaranteed paycheck. This is not a concept that is comfortable for many. I get that.

I wanted to change more than anything after I got this information placed in me. I never stopped learning after I was introduced to this type of genre. Here's the real kicker with personal growth—there is a knowing-doing gap. The leaders of this direct selling company were genius. They knew that by getting people to have the courage and confidence to sell, they first needed to get them to believe they could.

I sat in awe as I listened to the speakers at the seminars we went to. I craved going to these events as something inside me was waking up. I was beginning to feel alive. I listened intently to their success stories. I attempted everything they told me to do. I read books, listened to CDs, wanted more, and was hungry for a better life. And suddenly, that lion in the cage began to roar. It burned inside me, and I did not know how to get that lion outside of its cage.

It was then that I did start to take some risks. Although I knew all the steps, read all the books, and did all the things everyone recommended, I didn't realize that my own self-image was the one thing that was severely holding me back. I thought that I had figured it all out! I read the books to check them off the list, to say, "Yep, I read that one too," but I didn't realize that change doesn't come from knowing; it comes from doing the hard work. And doing the hard work on yourself first.

With that comes a ton of frustration, and with frustration comes a lot of excuses. "Well, I'm a single mom." "Well, I have to work, I don't have time. I'm not wired that way; these people had to have been born with a silver spoon in their mouths. That's meant for them, not for people like me." Blah blah blah. The speakers on stage were those who had the top sales in the company. They had great stories. I would listen intently as they told their own stories. Many of these stories included awful, broken, and sad pasts followed by a great personal success story. I identified, but I just could not get to the point of seeing myself in their position. I didn't understand then that the hard work began on the inside. I didn't improve how I spoke to myself. I still told myself that I was the class airhead. I still told myself that nobody would want me. I still told myself that I wasn't deserving of success. I still told myself that I was broken. So, because I didn't improve how I spoke to myself, I didn't tell myself a new story, and my circumstances never changed. To put it in simple terms, I had poor habitual behaviors. Consciously I wanted to do better, but my habits were still in line with what I felt I deserved. I acted in a manner of what I expected my results to be and what I believed I was worth.

After reading John Assaraf's book, *Innercise: The New Science to Unlock Your Brain's Inner Power*, I realized that my brain was doing its primary function of keeping me safe. This is precisely why I felt anxiety and fear anytime I wanted to change my poor habitual behaviors. When we do something that is out of our comfort zone, our brain will play tricks on us and give us a warning. The comfort zone is powerful, and our brain's primary function will keep us from being our best selves, if we don't train it otherwise.

I've also realized that fear and excitement are very similar feelings. I'd get excited about something, and immediately fear would set in. My desire would feel scary, or not worth the risk of putting myself out there, so I'd fall back into the comfort zone, and keep the lion inside caged. I had to change this. I had to know that my self-image, and what I believed I was worthy of, had to shift.

Changing the self-image is a *must* in order to change the behavior, and the only way to change the behavior is to commit to what it is you desire and *be* the person who has it already. We become so good at believing our own excuses of why we are unable to do something that we give ourselves an out before ever attempting to create the habit. This nonsense has got to stop if we want to accomplish anything. And I mean, anything! Are you a person who is reliable because you do what you say you will do, or do you begin with a victim mindset that comes with excuses? I assure you; I know this behavior all too well! My mantra was always, "Yeah, but." "Yeah, but I'm a single mom." "Yeah, but I don't have any money." "Yeah, but I don't want to upset anyone." The list went on and on, and I believed every single one of my "Yeah, buts" and fully believed that no one else understood. I believed my excuses were so good that I almost wore them as my badge of honor. I literally had an attachment to my excuses and not getting what I desired.

_Un_ CAGED

Victim or Victor?

The question that keeps the lioness tame—"Why can't I accomplish my dreams just like the people I look up to do?"

The question that sets her free— "What do I desire, and how do I become the kind of person who would accomplish this goal?"

ACTION STEPS

1. Think of a person in your life who has accomplished a goal that you desire.
2. Write down how this person acts. What do you admire about this person? How does this person dress? How does this person treat those around them? How do you imagine this person begins and ends his or her day? What are the habits this person had to implement before seeing this goal come into fruition?
3. Write down the daily habits you need to implement to be that kind of person.
4. What habits are prohibiting you from getting there?
5. Decide if you are committed to the goal or merely interested. When we are committed, we find a way. When we are interested, we find an excuse. If you are committed, move to step #6.
6. Commit and let nothing stand in your way of implementing those habits daily.

CHAPTER 5.
The Lies Must Be Destroyed

Until we destroy the old inner story, anything new is temporary.

I earned my real estate license in August of 2010, and I had my first closing the following January. That's right, do the math. I went five months without a paycheck. That would be five long months of paying for office supplies and rent, board dues, business cards, signs, etc. I had money going out everywhere! I had money going out that I did not have to spend.

When I took my first client out to look at homes, I didn't even know what a lockbox was or what it looked like. (This is what the house key is locked in, and only the realtor has the way in.) I had to

55

pretend that I knew what I was doing. Not only did I not know what a lockbox looked like, but I also didn't know how to open it. The listing agent gave me a code, and I didn't even know what that meant or what to do with it. I pulled through, somehow ended up getting that buyer under contract, and thought that I had won the lottery. That is until I looked at what I had spent so far. I looked at what my commission would be, what taxes had to be paid, and what the broker took as their split, and I realized I had spent more than what I'd make.

The saga continued. I told myself the story that I didn't know if I would make it in real estate after all. I waited tables in my own hometown when I first got my real estate license to make ends meet. Although I was very proud to have my real estate license, I was embarrassed to be back where I had begun. There's something I need to say—I loved serving tables. In fact, I'd do it again for the fun of it. It was my own self-image that told me I was appearing to my peers as taking another step back in life. Again, I was so damn worried about the opinions of others—silly me.

It was an unforgettable day when I was in the restaurant, working a lunch hour, and I walked out to see a voicemail from an agent in my office that I had looked up to. I thought this agent was one of the best of the best. And don't get me wrong, he was pretty darn good. He asked me if I wanted to join his team as a buyer's agent. He told me he had become too busy to handle all of the business he had and needed help. What a phenomenon this was to me! Too much work and he would mentor me and show me the ropes in real estate?! Count me in! What a blessing in disguise this was for me. He fulfilled all those promises, and I was eventually closing deals.

Three years later, I went solo, and once again, I found myself spending more money than I had made. According to NAR (The National Association of Realtors), 87% of realtors fail in the first five years. 87%! If you are not tenacious and have a big fat reason for sticking with it, the failure rates are against you.

I was nowhere near, what some would call, an overnight success. Comparatively speaking, I am not sure many would consider me a success at all (nasty little voice). However, success is relative, and if I'm doing what I set out to do, that's success in my book. I sold so few homes at the beginning that I believe that I had an income of zero on my taxes during the first two years of selling real estate alone. I had a few closings, but not enough to cover my expenses.

Why do I tell you this? I believe that we see people who have had any type of accomplishments in any area of life and we fail to realize the sacrifice it may have taken them to get there. I was simply willing to cry more than the average person, fail and fall on my face over and over, go without any extras, and scrounge pennies for way longer than most could fathom. Crazy? Very, very likely. But that damn lion would just not shut up. What we fail to realize is the struggle happening internally – the burning desire to fulfill a dream versus the fear of letting go of safety. Struggle was my safety. It's what I knew. It's how I programmed myself to believe it's what I deserved. Letting go of this meant acquiring a new internal identity and taking responsibility for where I was. Nothing can change unless we first take responsibility for where we are.

I love real estate, and this was it; I was going after it. The hard thing for me was that no matter how many homes I sold, I thought any success of mine must be a fluke. Some would say, "Oh, you have success," and I would think, "Oh my gosh, you don't even know what my bank account looks like." Others would say, "Can you teach me what you're doing?" and I would say, "Of course I will." And in my head, I would think, "Don't take my advice; I'm not that good." I'd compare my Chapter 1 to someone else's Chapter 20. I'd look at other realtors' social media posts and compare my ugly real-life parts to the parts of their lives that they made public. As with everything in life, success is relative! I was tenacious, I had a lion roaring inside of me, but I would still hold myself back with self-sabotaging self-talk.

When you climb to the top in business and in life, there will be others who want to be sure you don't outgrow them. I didn't only hear opinions of those who believed I had any kind of success (again relative); I also heard, "Oh, so now you're a big shot," and, "So now you're too good for us." And wouldn't you know it, my worst critic was me.

And again, the critic is what I listened to most. Why? Because my self-esteem wasn't going to allow me to truly find happiness in a small taste of accomplishment. My self-esteem was more comfortable with not being judged, so I'd talk small and play small to fit in. And in turn, my business would do the same. At this point of my career, I didn't realize that the old image of myself must be completely destroyed in order to BE the person who truly believed I was successful.

You'd never know it, though. I was really good at holding my head high and giving the illusion that my self-esteem was high; however, my self-esteem was not in line with my goals and dreams. I still spoke to myself like no one would ever speak to their worst enemy.

The story I told myself in my head was that any success I had was temporary. The story I told myself was that I didn't deserve it. And so once again, I must prove myself right with a bit of self-sabotage sprinkled on top of any ounce of success I had.

The real story is that I needed to find inner happiness before I could appreciate anything else. The real story is that although I could likely recite many self-help books and say all the right things, I had it completely backward. Without a positive self-image, none of this mattered. I'd continue to work hard, I'd continue to have a little bit of success, and I'd continue to lose it all.

It was three years into going solo in my career that the inner voice began to change and started to scream. It had no choice. I had to break up with the negative thoughts of who I was and start telling myself a new story. My biggest cheerleader (my mom) was not there any longer to remind me that I am capable of great things.

*Un*CAGED

Victim or Victor?

The question that keeps the lioness tame—"Why does my success always feel temporary?"

The question that sets her free—"What can be strengthened within me and within my business in order to achieve my goals?"

ACTION STEPS

1. If you knew that everything you needed to accomplish your dreams is already available to you, what would you desire to achieve? Write it down.

2. In as much detail as possible, list how accomplishing this goal would benefit your life.

3. List every fear that comes to mind. What could go wrong?

4. Imagine your best friend just told you that what you wrote down in step 1 was their goal, and then they followed it with all of the reasons you listed in step 3 as to why they weren't going to get after it.

5. Write down what you would say to them. What is your advice?

CHAPTER 6. *Mom*

When things change in an instant, we must learn to be resilient.

My mom, my rock, worked in the same office as I did. She worked at the in-office title company, and she, of course, was there to help me every step of the way. Every morning on my way to my office, I'd pass her office, say good morning to her, go back to my office, shut the door, and after about 15 minutes would pass, she'd sneak back to check on me. She'd come in making small talk, but she was often there to make sure that I had enough money to eat or offer me half of the lunch that she packed for herself. She made sure I could pay all of my bills, but frequently she'd suggestively say to me, "Oh Brooke, maybe a full-time, salary paid job is what you need." However, she knew that the only thing worse than being broke to me was not fulfilling the idea of being a successful Realtor.

I'm sure she worried about me way more than I knew, or more so about my children. And although she likely thought that a nine to five was the safer choice, she encouraged me every step of the way.

Every time I walked out of the office door, I would pass her office again. I'd let her know if I was going on a listing appointment, if I was going out with a buyer, or if I was simply going home to get my kids out of daycare and spend time with them. Every time I left the office, her words were filled with phrases such as, "You go girl," "Go get it," "You've got this," and "I believe in you," and nearly every night when she left for home, she would call me to ask how my appointments went. She was my cheerleader. She wanted me to succeed. She also desperately wanted to protect me and keep me safe. She worried about me. She worried about my children, not because she didn't believe in me, but because chasing a dream career was not something that she was familiar with. She also saw my cycle of having a small taste of success (selling a few homes) and losing it all.

This closeness between my mother and me was not a new thing. I'm the oldest daughter of four kids, and my mom was my person. We weren't perfect by any means! We had our own family disputes, and we had our own issues. But in comparison, I will tell you my upbringing was terrific. My mom lived for her family. Her kids were her everything, or at least we thought until the grandbabies came along. Oh, how she loved those babies!

It was a family full of love. It was a family that was loud. And to this day, we're all still extremely close.

Things change in an instant!

On January 13, 2015, our terrific, full of love, and loud family was turned upside down.

I was at a Detroit training for real estate when I got a surprise phone call at 8 a.m. The training was just beginning, so I didn't answer. My phone rang again. My husband at the time and I had an agreement that if we didn't answer the phone, all is good. We work. We're busy. But if we called twice, you had to answer it because it was important. He called twice, and I picked up to hear the words, "Your mom has been in a car accident." The person I rode with said, "We're leaving right now." We jumped in the car, and thankfully, we took her car, so I didn't drive. As I was in the passenger seat on the way home, I received many frantic, "Where are you?" phone calls. The two-hour trip to the hospital felt like an eternity. I ran in through the emergency room, and the staff was waiting for me at the door. They escorted me to the back room where I found my entire family, full of tears, and a priest. If you're not Catholic, allow me to inform you. When you see a priest, and someone's been in a car accident, you know things are not good.

I immediately went into hysterics; my dad wrapped his arms around me and said, "Yes, this is what we may be facing." I never had the chance to have another conversation with my mom. While we were in the hospital, I never saw her awake. In the beginning, I'd get a thumb rub while holding her hand, but I really don't remember the last conversation we had together.

After a week of hell, we lost our mom, we lost our queen bee. I lost my biggest supporter; I lost the one who kept me safe. I lost the one who knew all of my weaknesses yet still was my biggest cheerleader. She put me in my place when I needed it. She hated being in the spotlight, but I believe I get my boldness from her. She was not one to hold back when she had an opinion.

Most people will say that this is the worst thing that could have happened to a family, that we were robbed, didn't get to spend enough time with her, and that she was taken from us way too soon. They are right. It was awful. It was probably the worst thing I ever went through, but I am beyond grateful for the time that I had with my mom; I am beyond thankful that she was my mom. She came to this Earth for a purpose, and she fulfilled that purpose beautifully. We can't put a timeframe on that.

From this moment on, I had to figure out a new normal. My mom wasn't a part-time grandma or a mom that I spoke to once a week. She was my co-parent. She was a co-worker. She was who I depended on for, well, if I'm being honest, more likely than what most 30 somethings depend on their own moms for. It was a moment that would change me forever, and it was up to me to decide how.

After about eight months of deep grief, a lot of therapy, and a lot of self-discovery, something inside me changed. I no longer had my mom there to say to me, "You go, girl." "You've got this." "You are capable of great things." I no longer had anyone coming to my office to ensure that I was fed, that my children were taken care of, or that my lights would stay on. However, I still found myself speaking to her every day, and I would imagine what she would say to me then. Every time I would get in my car to go to a listing appointment, I would talk to her. I'd think about how she'd respond, and eventually, her voice became my inner voice. I found myself saying the same things to me that she would tell me. I became my own cheerleader; I became my own biggest fan. I became the person who believed in me. My inner voice was beginning to change.

After much personal growth, the need for change, and digging deep on looking for my purpose, I learned a few things. I learned that changing your story and your inner dialogue is what is most important. It is the story that we tell ourselves repeatedly, of which we become, and I needed a new story. When my mom was here, I was safe, and I knew I'd never fail. I'd always have food on my table, my lights would always stay on, and I'd always be loved unconditionally. As you will read in the next chapter, I was dependent on my mom and others for my own happiness. If we know our physical life on earth is temporary, what happens to our joy when it's dependent on a person filling our void if they are suddenly taken? This was something I needed to figure out, and fast.

I do have a family that looks out for each other, even without our mom here. We'd never let one person or another hit rock bottom, but she was my person. She was who I went to for everything. This was the wake-up call that I needed to grow up. I had to start telling myself a new story. I had to take responsibility for exactly where my life was.

Before my mom's death, I thought I had figured it all out. I'd already read the books. I had already attended the seminars. It was that knowing-doing gap that held me back. The doing comes from what we believe we are worth. If we feel we are worth something, we will become that person naturally. If you want something but hold back, it's a direct reflection of your self-image. No excuse can stop you if you know this to be true. It is only the action that will bring you results. Talk is cheap, but when you feel something in your soul and know your worth, your actions will show it every time.

I believe we all have a purpose. I don't believe in coincidences, and I honestly don't really believe in accidents either. I think my mom had an incredible purpose, and I think that she fulfilled her purpose beautifully. Her effect on all who knew her is different. I'll never know the level of an effect she had on her seven sisters and one brother; I'll never know the effect she had on my very own siblings, my father, those she knew as a child, or her adult relationships. But this is what I do know, if you knew her, you loved her. Her purpose was incredible – her smile and her laugh were contagious, and she brought a smile to all who knew her. The stories I hear now of her positive effect on others are fun to listen to. If you don't believe you have a purpose, think again, my friend.

"There is a purpose for everyone you meet. Some people come into your life to test you, some to use you, and some to bring out the very best in you." - Author Unknown

Be the person who brings out the very best in others.

Of course, I feel robbed of my mom's short time here on Earth. I think about how she lived her life, and I wonder if she would have done anything differently knowing her time here would be short. Then I think that we may not have tomorrow promised to us. Actually, we don't. Tomorrow is never promised. What would I change? I dug deep into this topic.

My mom's sudden passing was one of several sudden losses I experienced in a short period of time. It was just a month before her death that my boisterous, fun, and loving 29-year-old cousin suddenly passed. I come from a very large Catholic family, have over 50 first cousins (between both families), and this is a family full of love and fun. This was a loss that no family should have to go through. In a matter of one month, my grandma lost a child and a grandchild. In a matter of one month, my aunt lost a son and a sister. My father lost his wife, and days later, a new grandbaby would be born that would never know his grandma. It was a short three months after my mom's death that we said goodbye to my grandma, my father's mom. In a matter of a few months, my entire family, as we knew it, was changed forever.

Two years after my mom passed, I sat alone with my high school best friend, my fellow high school cheerleader, and the most positive person I knew as she took her last breath. She lost her horrific battle to cancer, leaving two small children, a husband, her mother, and many who loved her behind.

The grieving process began again. I am no stranger to tragic and sudden loss. I had the option to become angry (which I was for some time) and stay there or look at the many blessings they all provided and honor them by living fully.

Most of us live to keep others, even strangers, happy, and we listen to their advice, even if they don't have what we want. I don't think we do this purposefully. I believe we do it because it's what we know. We become a product of our environments, and we justify why we aren't entirely fulfilled. We are trained to believe that a dream-life is "Either for other people," or "It's selfish, or crazy, to want more than we're blessed with now."

So, let me give you permission to get after it. Why? I believe that those I love, and whom I lost suddenly, would tell us to live fully.

I now believe it's selfish to live in comfort and not chase your passion. Living without listening to that inner voice is what's selfish. You know that inner voice that tells you when something isn't right? Yep, that voice! That voice that says you're here for a reason, the one that says, "You have a purpose." Listen to it. I believe that we come here not to just exist but to make a difference, whether in one life or in many lives. I believe that our Creator made each of us unique, all with an individual purpose, and I think that we have an earthly experience to evolve, learn those lessons, and make a difference. The ones that changed the world, or the life of someone else, are the ones who went after it, got really uncomfortable, were ridiculously brave, listened to their inner voice, and had the self-image that they were worthy. They found their passion; they let nothing else get in the way.

"Your talent is God's gift to you. What you do with it is your gift back to God. What are you doing with your talent today?" - Leo Buscaglia

Victim or Victor?

The question that keeps the lioness tame—"Why would God take those I love away from me?"

The question that sets her free—"What can I learn from this tragic loss, and how can I positively impact others through this?"

ACTION STEPS:

When we feel joy, we are in complete alignment with our spirit. The feeling of joy is how we find our purpose. We are meant to enjoy our journey, so find joy along the way! If this is difficult, follow these action steps:

1. Write down something you enjoyed doing in the past but stopped doing.

2. Describe, in detail, how spending your time on that brought you joy.

3. Describe how it either directly, or indirectly, brought joy to others.

4. Finding our purpose is really just asking ourselves, "What can I do with my time that is important?" What can you implement to bring this joyful activity back into your life?

5. What activities are you willing to give up and replace this with?

CHAPTER 7. *Relationships*

For us to give love, we must first love ourselves.

Although this story isn't about my specific relationships, it is about what I told myself while in them. Remember, I told myself I was broken, and my self-image was not always high.

I've felt swept off my feet, and, of course, have been excited about relationships. I've also been great at ignoring red flags and not listening to my inner spirit telling me something is not right. I've chosen the need to be loved over doing what was right for me. Now I know, we attract what we think about most. I have been insecure enough to not be 100% my authentic self; therefore, I couldn't be emotionally

75

available and didn't listen to my intuition. Unauthentic and emotionally unavailable? Yep, I've attracted that.

I have been disconnected in some relationships, with little depth and no passion. This I know—I wanted a partner except I didn't know how to be the best version of me for a partner.

I'm going to be very transparent here. I've been in a really ugly relationship. A relationship that was so toxic I lost friends over it and had family worried sick about me. I was too blind and broken down to see it at the time. Unfortunately, this relationship taught me that vulnerability equals the ability for the one who is supposed to love you most to tear you down and throw all insecurities back in your face. When we learn, by allowing it, that vulnerability means pain, heartbreak, and verbal abuse, we become hard, surfaced, and don't allow others to see us as our true, authentic selves. For me, years after this relationship ended, I became severely lonely, even if I were in a relationship. I'd allow others to see small parts, the parts I wanted to be seen, and felt that this meant strength. I now know that strength is allowing yourself to be seen. I now understand that vulnerability, with those who earn it, is powerful. I'm still getting comfortable with the idea that vulnerability can also mean connection. Actually, if you're not dealing with an asshole, that's exactly what it should mean.

I add this to the book to say that I totally get it that being vulnerable is ridiculously scary. I decided, after many, many years, that this would not debilitate me any longer. With this decision, I did experience pain again, and I take the chance of experiencing it many times over. The decision to be vulnerable comes with the conscious knowledge that pain may be a part of it—I can accept this, as I now understand that I have zero control over what someone else may do.

To learn to love oneself is also to be your authentic, true self. When we are authentic, we attract those who appreciate our truth. To love ourselves is also to enjoy our own company. This, my friends, is powerful! Why? Because let's face it, loneliness is a bitch! Allow me to be clear here, being alone and being lonely are not the same. Start discovering your great self, learn to love her, and give her grace.

Discovering myself has made me aware of the type of people I want to allow in my life, and I am not only talking about romantic relationships. It taught me that it's not my job to change people. It's not my job to give them excuses for their behavior either. It taught me to set boundaries and that if I put up with nonsense from the beginning, I should expect to put up with it over and over. It taught me to love myself enough to say "goodbye" and make room for the people who deserve me.

Should we need a partner? Likely not. Is it okay to want one? Hell yes! Allow me to explain. We must ask ourselves, "Do I want to be in a relationship because it fills a void, or do I want this relationship because it enhances my human experience?" When we look to others to fill a void within us, we are putting unfair pressure on another person. Our own happiness cannot be dependent on what another human does or says. We must be so solid with who we are that we don't need a void filled. This inner joy attracts the company of folks who don't put the pressure of *their* happiness on you. Ouch! I know, I learned this the hard way too.

Loving yourself enough to not *need* to be in a relationship is the best thing you can do for those who love you. I'm a firm believer that it's nearly impossible to fully love others if you don't love yourself first. Relying on someone else for your happiness is not love; it's dependency. Being with someone for the sake of not being alone will not bring joy. Give yourself, and those who love you, the best gift possible—learn to love yourself and take the pressure of *your* happiness off of your loved ones.

This does not mean you don't care when they're down. It doesn't mean that you're not there to talk to. It simply means that their bad moment doesn't have control over your own joy (and vice versa). That's when true connection begins.

"Connection is why we're here; It is what gives purpose and meaning to our lives." - Brené Brown

I no longer depend on others to fill a void I have within me. I also now have the strength to ask for what I deserve and say no to what does not feel right - this sometimes means that relationships change or end. Every relationship has an unspoken agreement; therefore, if you outgrow that agreement, state it, and set a different boundary, the relationship may need to end. Unless, of course, the other person grows with you.

I've learned to get in tune with my inner spirit, and I now understand that I am loved unconditionally, by a higher power greater than any human could ever give. That pressure is now off anyone who comes my way, and the ones who enhance my life most are the ones who appreciate this. Solid people attract other solid people, and what a powerful experience that makes. Rather than looking to others to fulfill a void, I'm able to look at my life and ask, "What story am I telling myself about my worth based on these results?"

Victim or Victor?

The question that keeps the lioness tame—"Why can't I find a relationship that makes me happy?"

The question that sets her free—"What do I need to fix internally to find joy without looking for another human to fill that void?"

ACTION STEPS:

1. Think of the most valuable relationships in your life.
2. Write down, in detail, what your self-image is when you are around the person who you feel most joy with.

   - How would this person describe you?

3. Write down, in detail, what your self-image is when you are around the person you feel most angst with.

   - How would this person describe you?

4. Write down what you love about yourself.
5. Our lives /relationships are a mirror of our own self-image - write down one thing you can do this week to improve your self-image.

CHAPTER 8. *Boundaries*

Learn who deserves our attention and who does not.

Since I'm on the subject of relationships, I want to address something I've learned that may just be one of my hardest lessons to date.

I did not know how to set boundaries for myself. I was terrified of upsetting someone at the beginning of any relationship—whether it be a friendship, a job, or a romantic relationship. I told myself I was a people-pleaser when, in reality, I was simply a self-sabotager.

When someone shows you who they are, believe them! I'd put a smile on my face for fear of coming across as a bitch or a nag, say nothing, and then wonder why I was so frustrated or blindsided when things went wrong. Think about some of my real-life examples and ask yourself if any apply to your own life:

- I've engaged in gossip and then felt blindsided when those same people would gossip about me.
- I've helped men pull out of debt at the beginning of relationships, to my own detriment, and then couldn't believe there was a spending issue.
- I've accepted positions that offered me way less than I was worth and then became frustrated for feeling underpaid.
- I've loved a great challenge, the chase, and the game at first, and then wondered why or how some partners were emotionally unavailable.

Boundaries. Yep, that's a tough one for many. I'd dare say it may be even more challenging for us women who have strong personalities and ambitions but fear coming across as a bitch.

You are not a bitch for knowing your worth.

Relationships end, become toxic, or lack trust due to the tough conversations we avoid. Have the conversation. Set your boundaries. If something doesn't "feel" right, it's not! Avoiding the conversation or thinking you may change the person, be the exception, or that you somehow deserve to be treated poorly will make you miserable and likely just prolong the ending anyway. Setting healthy boundaries for yourself frees you up to have healthy relationships. Not only that, it gains respect from those who are strong enough to handle your truth. These are the people we want in our lives anyway, aren't they?

I'm a visual person, so let me explain how I see this. I think of my hand in a fist when I try to *grip* onto an outcome that I desire yet have no control over. We have no control over other people's actions. Zero! So instead, don't grip. Release the control. Our hands must be open to receive. Be open to receiving what you deserve rather than gripping onto an outcome that you have no control over. We only have control over what we are willing to put up with. Everyone has their shit. What shit are you willing to deal with?

Since we teach people how to treat us, could the feeling of continuously being treated poorly be from a lack of set boundaries from the beginning?

Knowing your worth and allowing yourself to stop the judgment of yourself (you know, the inner voice who says, "You're not worthy") is also a reflection of how you will see others. What we judge in others is a reflection of what we judge in ourselves. Stop the judgment of yourself, celebrate you, and become ready to celebrate others as well. Easy? No way! I have failed on this many, many times, and I will continue to do so. Being aware of what you judge about yourself, and others, is a painful first step. It brought more judgment of myself at first; I really didn't like some parts of me that I knew needed to change. Change at first is extremely difficult, which is why I believe most avoid it at all costs. Be brave enough to make the change. The other side is a powerful one.

With that said, we need to be able to set boundaries; we need to allow ourselves the power to say, "This does not feel good; therefore, I'm not going there." Or, "This does not work for me." And we have to allow ourselves to be able to say that without feeling guilty about it. We have to be able to have the inner strength to say, "This is not okay." Whether or not you (or they) are doing something wrong is irrelevant. It doesn't matter who is right or who is wrong. If it does not feel right or does not sit well with you, it is important to say so.

Here's an example: Think about whether or not you've ever felt blown off. Somebody will say, "Hey, can we reschedule?" at the very last minute and have to change plans, cancel altogether, or not show up when they're supposed to. Some are just not there emotionally the way you are for them. I acknowledge that things happen. I'm not speaking of the unusual situations that this can come up with. You're a smart cookie—at least your inner being is. Listen to it when it says, "This is not okay."

These are behaviors that I would continuously put up with, and allow me to say, not from bad people. We teach people how to treat us. So, what would happen is I would say, "Sure, no problem. Absolutely. I can reschedule," and what I was really saying is, "I have no problem rearranging my entire day to accommodate what it is that you need. I'll put myself and my family out to avoid you being upset with me, leaving me, or having a conflict." And whether or not this is with a family member, a friend, a partner, a spouse, or at work, we build resentment when we continue to do this.

When we don't have boundaries, days, weeks, and sometimes years down the road, we look at our lives and ask, "Why does this person treat me that way? Why is this person unreliable? Why is this person treating me in a manner that does not feel good?" Allow me to say that the answer to that is because the boundaries weren't set in the first place, and sister, I don't say this lightly. This is a lesson I learned way too late. It's a lesson I will work on until the day I die, because as a woman, as a human, I believe that many of us have found our worth through the acceptance of others. Most of us will do anything to get that. I'll repeat it; we teach people how to treat us.

Be brave and know your worth! You are worth only beautiful things, and what we look for is exactly what we find. If we believe others will treat us unworthy, we will find that too. I promise you, what you expect, what you think you deserve, is what you will find—every time. Perhaps not on your ideal timeframe, but every time.

Sometimes it's painful. And sometimes people will walk away. And sometimes they don't like what you have to say, and that's okay. Growing can sometimes feel like we are breaking at first—as with all things, this too is temporary.

Knowing my boundaries and sticking true to what feels right for me has been a game-changer in every relationship I now have. It's not easy, but it is empowering. I still mess it up frequently, but now I can look at my life as a reflection of my own self-esteem and say, "This is an area I must work on. This is an area that I must set boundaries." Boundaries are set by those who know they're worth great things and don't put up with less. Am I suggesting we be selfish? YES! That's precisely what I'm suggesting. If you don't set boundaries for yourself, prepare to be walked on. This is not the fault of those who walk on you. It's simply because you allow it.

Everyone will have an opinion on how you handle your business. I am not interested in everyone's opinion. Have I been before? Oh, sister, so much so that it would stop me from being confident in my own thoughts. I would seek approval in every way I could. Now that I've learned this lesson (eh hem, the hard way), some people just don't get the satisfaction of me worrying about what their opinion is of me. Do not, I repeat, do not allow the opinions of everyone to matter to you. There will always be naysayers, those who want to bring you down while you're at the top, those who feel insignificant in their own lives and take it out on you, etc. These behaviors have zero to do with you and 100% to do with them. Can it still hurt? Absolutely! But we've got to find a way to not let other's judgments of us debilitate our worth. Do not grip onto the idea of changing them, their behavior, or their opinion. We cannot make everyone happy, so let's not even try. Keep those hands open to receive those who are meant for you and stop gripping onto those and the things that aren't.

Here's a real-life example of this. I mentored an agent who had a client he adored. As time passed, he had done several real-estate deals with this family, but there was a specific transaction that was different. He told me his client began to believe that he owed her more than she was getting. He was beginning to be treated as if she was doing him a favor and his services were not enough to justify the repeat business. He complained multiple times that this was affecting him greatly in all areas of his life. His client would text him unkind words, then apologize and act like his best friend. When things didn't go exactly as she thought they would during the listing period of her house, she proceeded to say unkind things about him publicly on social media. He felt it was extremely hurtful and passive-aggressive. After observing him go through so much hurt, I had to finally say to him, "You've got to let this go. You have to expire this listing."

Some may consider this a weak move. Oh, my friend, this took great strength. The old me would have told him to justify his worth, hold on to this for dear life, and prove himself to exhaustion. I did find myself saying this for a minute, but when I realized it was robbing him of his own happiness, along with soaking up his energy and depriving him of looking for the good in all other parts of his business, it was time for him to say goodbye.

After time had passed, this agent and I reflected on this situation. Due to the history he had with this client, and a super soft spot in his heart for this family, he doted over her immensely. After reflection, he realized he didn't set boundaries from the beginning. He put up with being treated poorly and didn't expect that it would continue. His biggest regret was not having the hard conversation up front.

What sometimes appears to be the weakest decision is the decision that takes the most strength. If you're coming from a place of love, and someone is pushing your boundaries and stealing your positive energy, it's time to let it go. No amount of money, energy, or precious time is worth compromising the boundaries you've worked so hard to set in place.

_Un_**CAGED**

Victim or Victor?

The question that keeps the lioness tame—"Why do people treat me poorly?"

The question that sets her free—"What areas of my life do I need to set boundaries in so that my worth is respected?"

ACTION STEPS:

1. Write down any resentment, anger, or discomfort you are feeling about a person or situation.

2. Write down and be clear about what you desire the outcome to be.

3. Write your answer of step 2 again and become emotionally involved in that outcome.

4. Prioritize your feelings and desires. What do you need to say no to?

5. Write down your options and take action.

6. Expect resistance and know that is okay.

CHAPTER 9. *Therapy*

Yep, I'm going there. The taboo subject that must be talked about.

Can we talk about therapy? I need to tell you that therapy is something that not only the broken need. It is my opinion that therapy is needed for everybody. We all have ugly. We all make mistakes; we all tell ourselves a story. And sometimes we have to be able to talk those out. Sometimes, speaking about it out loud is what helps when we're stuck in the ugly negativity of our own minds. We can only make sense of what we know at the time. In my own experience, there have been moments that I'd hide the real truth to protect other people. On the flip side of that, there were times I wouldn't speak about my own pain because I didn't want anyone to worry about me. Therapy allows us to be able to speak to a non-bias person. And it allows that person to be able to come with a new perspective. In fact, most of the time, I'd just need to speak out loud about what I was thinking and how I was feeling.

Therapy, for me, comes in all forms. Sometimes it's wine night with the girls; other times, it's taking a walk, talking to your pastor, exercise, a phone call to someone you love, a Hallmark movie, meditation, etc. In simple terms, therapy is putting you first for a moment and figuring out the hard shit.

I don't think professional therapy is something that we need to do all the time, but there have been situations in my life where I had to talk to somebody. The first time I saw a professional was when I was a single mom living with my parents, and I could not figure out how to break through from the cycle of dating the wrong men and feeling like my life was going nowhere, and the thought that I was still stupid was a booming one at this time. The negative self-talk was brutal. I had to get a different perspective because my self-talk was not helping my situation.

The other time that I was in therapy was with my ex-husband. This was not a marriage that we threw away lightly. Divorce is awful. Neither of us wanted it. We tried for years. We had been in therapy several times. I'll never forget the time I had a session on my own and my therapist looked at me and said, precisely this, "Brooke, you demand so much of yourself, your business, your reputation, etc. Why do you not require the same for those you allow into your life?" Allow me to be clear here—he was not suggesting that I have the power to change others, or even demand great things of others. He was asking me to think about what I expect for myself in regard to all of my relationships. He was suggesting I think about who I am, what I desire and expect for my life, and how to get both in alignment. Perhaps he was even suggesting that there was a void inside me that I must fix, as another human will never live up to the demand of filling a void for me. Let me tell you, that is a hard lesson. It took years and years of me trying to unfold this exact question. Although I still work on it, this is where the topics of setting boundaries and learning to love myself came to play.

The other time that I went to therapy was when my mom passed away. At the end of that horrific week, we had to call in Hospice. Hospice is an incredible program. Hospice not only offers comfort to those who are passing but also provides comfort for the survivors. They offered grief therapy, which I grabbed on to and dove all in on. I knew I had to work this out. My mom passed suddenly, and although she was the most incredible mom that anyone could ask for, I had some shit that I had to get through. We are all imperfectly human. This means when she passed, I had some unfinished business that I needed to work through. I also had to work through my anger of feeling like she was stolen from us way too early. I had to work through the anger and the ability to forgive the man who accidentally hit her. I had to work through some of my own guilt.

I would sit with my therapist for hours. Grief therapy was different than what I had previously known. The therapist would sit with me, let me be, and be present with me the entire time. I give credit to that time in therapy for me to be able to run through grief. I still grieve my mom, but I am no longer stuck in grief. When we deal with the problem, rather than avoid it, when we face it head-on, when we do the hard work and talk about all of the painful things, we can move to the other side. There is no timeframe for grief, and it's entirely different for everyone. This process just allowed me to go through the phases and not stay stuck in one.

Don't ever be ashamed to want to go and talk to somebody. It's crucial. And for me, it is why I was capable to move past some things. I am human—I have love, I have guilt, I have pain, I hold resentment. And sometimes that really nasty inner voice comes creeping back in. It's healthy to allow yourself to be seen by a professional. I also would like to point out that not all therapists will be your match. And that's okay too. There are all different types of personalities. There are all different types of help out there. Whatever you find to be your therapy, do it.

I See You

Let's talk about the importance of being able to see others. We tend to want to be with people who are like us. When we go through periods of difficulty, I'll call them transitional points of life, we tend to surround ourselves with people who understand and who just *get it*.

When I went through my divorce, I wanted to talk to other people that had been through a divorce. I wanted a new perspective; I wanted to know that I was going to be okay. I wanted to know that the guilt that I felt was normal. I needed to know that the grieving process was healthy. I grabbed on to people who understood. I also did the same thing when my mom passed, especially at the beginning, because people don't know what to say in a situation like that. And I want to just tell you right now, the best thing to say is, "I don't know what to say. But I'm right here with you." The people who understood my grief were the ones who did just that. They sat with me and just let me grieve. They understood. They had empathy. They didn't try to make it right because they knew there was no way to do so.

Victim or Victor?

The question that keeps the lioness tame—"Why does my life seem to be falling apart?"

The question that sets her free—"What can I do for myself today that will help me move through this pain?"

*Un*CAGED

ACTION STEPS

1. Know that you are worth not living in pain and without guilt.

2. Find what makes you happy and spoil yourself.

3. Do something kind for you—spoil yourself.

4. Did I say to spoil yourself? Spoil yourself. Girl, you are worth it!

5. Know that therapy looks different for everybody. Find someone who gets it and ask them to coffee. If you're feeling like no one in your world does understand, make an appointment with a professional. Whatever you do, love yourself enough to know that you don't have to stay hurt.

CHAPTER 10. *Own Your Story.*

Without vulnerability, there is no true connection.

I look at these specific times of my life and think about everything I have gone through. I am not naive. I know my story is not bad in comparison to what many other people go through. I don't want to minimize that. I don't want it to seem like I've overcome these huge obstacles or that I believe I'm special because of it.

Every single person on this Earth is going through something. This is what I want you to get from this. We have to own our stories and be vulnerable to connect with other people who are going through life changes.

When I had this realization, my business changed. I looked at people differently, and my relationships changed. I could connect on a deeper level. First and foremost, I had to own my story. And there was some gruesome shit that needed to be worked out. And most of that was simply the story I was telling myself in my head. My own self-image had to be sorted out.

After the eight-month fog of deep, deep grief over my mom's loss, I called everyone in my entire database and apologized for not checking in and being present with them for that time. Because I was real and owned my position of where my business was, the conversations were real, authentic, and empowering. Did I need to apologize for grieving my mother? Hell no. But I did need to take responsibility for not giving my clients, my friends, and those I care about the attention they so deserve.

After the eight-month fog was lifted, my heart was so full. I was able to look back and see the sacrifice that others had made to help me through this time. Many Realtors in my office took time away from their own businesses and families to step up and help keep my business moving.

I was able to see others who were also grieving my mom's loss. I could get out of my own bubble and become grateful for the love, support, and sacrifice that so many had made. I acknowledged the amount of people who showed up to her funeral (we're talking thousands), those who prepared meals, those who were a listening ear, and those who didn't know what to say or do, but showed up anyway.

My vulnerability allowed others to see me exactly where I was. It allowed them to feel comfortable coming to me when they were hurting. It allowed them to ask me about my relationship with my mom rather than avoid what could have been an uncomfortable conversation for them.

I realized the importance of just showing up. I started to pay attention to what others were going through. I began going to more funerals; I wasn't afraid to call and simply say, "I see you" when I found out someone was going through real-life stuff. I started sending baby gifts to those who were celebrating a new life. I simply cared and realized the importance of saying so. I didn't do this to grow my business but to simply connect. But my business did change.

So how did my business change? It grew to the point that I needed help. I could not do the number of transactions I had without an assistant. Owning my story and seeing other people for where they were is what naturally grew my business.

"Every Move Has a Story"

Every Move Has a Story is my business tagline. Let me explain that. Anytime someone moves homes, it is always because of a life-changing event. This could be due to getting married, going through a divorce, a growing family, becoming an empty nester, having to sell a parent's home, dealing with a death, dealing with the relocation of a job, etc. You name it, there is a change; whether or not it's positive, neutral, or a change they don't want, there is a story behind every move. It is a vulnerable moment in someone's life. To be effective, I needed to look at my clients and say, "I'm right here with you, and I understand." Although no two stories are identical, owning my own story allows me to be more empathetic and caring to my clients.

People don't remember how well the transaction went. They expect the transaction to go smoothly—this is why they hire a professional. But people remember how we make them feel. To be a useful person, I had to get really clear on my own story. And I had to stop being ashamed of it. I had to own it. If I don't own my story, I don't give other people permission to own theirs. If I don't talk about the hurt and the pain that I went through at moments of my life, I don't allow somebody to come to me with their hurt and pain. If I can't celebrate all of the good things that are happening to me and for me, I don't allow people to come to me with their celebratory and happy moments. Being authentic and being vulnerable is what brings connection.

I decided that was the type of business I wanted. This is the type of life I wanted to live. From that point forward, my business changed. I made the decision that my business was not about the transaction. That's the easy part. That's expected. My business is about seeing people and knowing where they are. Sitting down with them and saying, "I understand. I'm here." That's all they want. That's all we want. As humans, we want to connect, and it is my job to not forget that there is a story every time there is a move.

I decided I wouldn't just be this way in business; I decided this is how my life had to look. I'll take the criticism, I'll be vulnerable, I'll put myself out there, and I won't worry (for long) about those who criticize it. I'll set boundaries to avoid feeling resentful to those I let in. Why? Because my relationships became much more fulfilled in comparison to when I hid who I was—when I was ashamed of my story. When I owned it, my connections became real. The relationship with myself had to change first, and when this happened, I allowed others to see me exactly as I am. This is the freest of all feelings!

Losing Myself in My Idea of Success

"I love it when you are too busy to talk! It's always a good sign." This text is what my college best friend, who still is to this day, sent me after I let her know I was, once again, working and couldn't chat. Mind you, it was a Saturday morning; I was in a panic to get to my appointment on time, and I had several meetings following.

Now, this particular friend, she meant it. If she thought that made me happy, she was on board. But for me? I had to ask myself, "Is this a good sign?" Is it a good sign that I have taught my peers to cheer me on because my definition of success is "too busy to talk"? I sat there and thought long and hard on this.

How many times have I sent a text that read, "Sorry, too busy. Catch ya later." Have I done this to my kids? Have I blown off relationships? Did I say this to my mom at all before she passed? Of course, I have! Of course, I did!

I just said it to my best friend. She is not an exception. Is this what I define as success? Is it only me? Good try.

Now, don't get me wrong, I'm in an industry that we work nights and weekends. And I LOVE my industry. But when we set our sights on a huge goal, we had better ask ourselves, "What is the WHY behind what I'm pushing so hard for?" and we damn well better stay true to that.

105

If you're not sure what I mean by *the why*, allow me to give my definition of it. A big why is the reason we do what we do. Without a big reason for it, we will either give up on our dream or lose who we are along the way. For example, if I say that my big why is to earn an income that allows me to provide a life for my children full of experiences, I had better learn how to be present and provide those experiences.

I'm naturally competitive. I like to win. I have a strong personality, and now, if I set my mind to something, I go for it. I will always have big goals. That's what keeps me ticking. Moving toward something and expanding is what gets me excited about living. I'm asking you to live an extraordinary life but by your own definition and no one else's.

In real estate and business, in general, when we find ourselves too busy to service our clients at a high level, we hire leverage. When leading others, the vision must be crystal clear in order for them to buy-in. Let me explain:

1. I'd dare say I've had some of the best people on the planet working in my organization. I would not have been able to function or run my business nearly as effectively without them.

2. Hiring people for the purpose of growth, managing a ginormous team, and eventually replacing myself was not my dream. It is what my coaches did, it is what they were coached to do, it was their dream, so this is what they taught me. Not once, but 10s of thousands of dollars in coaching sessions later. If this is your dream and you feel it in your bones, I want you to chase this as if your life depends on it. But for me, "Go bigger, go faster, do more, and don't breathe" is what I heard when my business coaches first asked me about my goals. They then gave me "their" blueprint of getting there, and so that's precisely what I attempted. I did it at the expense of my own happiness and my own sanity. The standard blueprint did not fulfill my purpose. It didn't fill my cup. It wasn't my path. My path did not require me to build a huge Real Estate team. My path is to tell my story and to help others see greatness within themselves. Until I was asked, "What do you desire?" and thought about it, I didn't know, and I was following the status quo.

Does this mean I can't have it all? ? Absolutely not. It simply meant the path needed to change. The vision was clear, and my team was clearly communicated with, so they had the confidence to take some detours with me. The goal never changes, but sometimes the path to get there must.

I'm a good student. Okay, you know better than that by now. But after all the work I've done, if I see something I want, I go to the person who has it, and I say, "Teach me, I'm all in." Those I asked to coach and mentor me were the ones doing the work I'd dreamt of— selling real estate, coaching, speaking, and inspiring others to be their best selves. I knew I wanted their results!

Having a coach, a mentor, and someone who can hold you accountable is, in my opinion, crucial as an entrepreneur. Hire the coach! Be clear on your intention, be open to discovering things about yourself, and have the strength to say, "This is not my path," if you find that it's not. Years into having a coach and working toward creating a big team, I learned that the particular path I was on was not one that brought me joy. I knew there had to be a different path. Not a different dream, just a different path of getting there. The hard part for me was defining exactly what I wanted from the start. Without being clear on this, I was willing to go down a path that others thought was best for me. It's not until we are clear on what we desire that we can then ask, "what's my next best step."

Here was my wake-up call—yep, you guessed it, another lesson taught from the passing of my mom. My mom was just about at retirement age when she was in her accident. She worked many long hours and would often say, "I can't wait to retire and be at the cottage." Am I saying don't work?! Absolutely not! But what I am saying is that we better enjoy the journey of getting to our destination. There is always, always, a different path. Be brave enough to find it, for you are not promised tomorrow. The "I'll be happy when" needs to stop now. Enjoy the journey! If you don't, keep the goal, but go a different way.

The path less traveled is often times the best path. Be brave enough to make your own path. Accountability, training, and being coached were essential to my growth, but let's first be sure the path is one you are excited about. Be brave enough to interview your coaches and have a say in which path they will coach you.

Victim or Victor?

The question that keeps the lioness tame—"Why try? I don't like what I'm doing."

The question that sets her free—"What do I need to change so that I can find joy in my journey?"

ACTION STEPS

1. List three things you do on a daily basis.

2. Next to each activity you listed, write down what is joyful for you within that activity. What is the sacrifice and what is the reward?

   Examples:

   - I don't always love prospecting for new business, but I find great joy in landing a listing appointment.

   - I don't always love cooking, but I find great joy in knowing that my family has nutritious meals.

   - I don't always like getting up early to hit the gym, but I find great joy in knowing my body is strong.

Consider this question, "How do I know if I need to find a different path?" I do believe we can find joy in everything, but if the bad outweighs the good, love yourself enough to make a change. Be careful not to confuse being afraid of making a change vs. seeking what is joyful. Here's an example.

   - My boss screams at me, my back hurts from the work I do, and I don't make enough money. No joy? It may be time for a tough conversation or the search for something new. Write down any activity that needs to change. What is one thing you can do this week to take action?

CHAPTER 11.

What Do You Desire?

The most important question that most do not know the answer to.

It's amazing to me how life will come full circle at times. I was having a holiday party for my team at a local restaurant and ran into the gentleman that took me on his real estate team. We hadn't spoken for several years, not for any particular reason, but life had happened, and we didn't stay connected. We decided to have coffee, and my life was forever changed (again) from that moment.

This gentleman had become a certified coach for Bob Proctor. If you're not familiar, watch "The Secret." I had seen the movie, and I

111

knew exactly who Bob was. I believed in the Law of Attraction (you've read many examples of it if you've made it this far in the book), and I was impressed to see the changes this gentleman made in his business, his personal life, and his energy as a whole. Once again, I said to him, "Show me what you're doing." And once again, he did.

I was introduced to a program that I so desperately needed. It was the perfect timing. I had been through real life, I had seen a touch of achievement, my kids were getting older, and I had to start thinking about what I really desire for my life after both my kids leave my home. It hit me hard that it would not be long before this would happen. What is it that I wanted life to look like? The main question he asked me is, "What do you desire?" How many of us have really asked ourselves this? What is it we desire?

I knew that in order for me to implement this coaching program into my day, I would need to rearrange my day. I told myself I had no extra time and that my energy was depleted, and I asked myself, how on earth would I fit one more thing in? When we ask good questions, our inner spirit leads us to the answer. I then recalled another book I had read (yep, to check it off the list, but again, not implement). This was the answer. I picked up *The Miracle Morning* by Hal Elrod and discovered how I'd fit in the pursuing my dreams into my schedule. My mornings now begin hours before the rest of the world wakes up.

I now study, visualize, meditate, keep a gratitude and affirmation journal, hold an exercise schedule, write, and most important of all, surround myself with folks who do the same (that's right, 6:30 a.m. group coaching calls). I continue to work on the coaching program diligently and put my big dreams to fruition. I complete all of it by 7 a.m., as I am unwilling to take away from my kids or my career, and not one of those priorities needs me before 7 a.m. This was the game-changer.

My cup is full before 7 a.m. I now pour into myself before I even say "Good morning" to another person. My cup is overflowing. My energy is through the roof. If you have no more to give, this is precisely why you need a routine of filling your cup!

This coaching program helped me understand that it was my self-image holding me back and stopping me from *really* pursuing my dreams. My inner self-image needed to strengthen in order for me to not only ask myself what it is that I want, but to also visualize me living my dreams and believing I'm worth them coming true—to know that I have a purpose. My self-image will need to strengthen again and again and again with every new phase of life I enter.

I looked back at journals I had written in at least five years before starting this program. My goals never changed. My inner being had the same desires. I just never had the self-confidence or the push to really go for them. This book was one of those goals. This book began once I got coached on how to discover my own paradigms. This is how I discovered that it was me, and only me, that was holding me back. That my life today is a mirror reflection of my self-image. It was then that I discovered ways to change my inner dialogue. I'm grateful for the business coaches I had, but this program was the one I needed most.

We cannot know what holds us back until we know ourselves. I encourage you to be selfish. I encourage you to discover this for you. We cannot understand why we are the way we are until we understand our own paradigms.

The following is one of the most powerful lessons I have learned to date. This powerful program, "Thinking into Results," by Bob Proctor and Sandy Gallagher teaches this about paradigm:

"Paradigms are a multitude of habits that guide every move you make. They affect the way you eat, the way you walk, even the way you talk. They govern your communication, your work habits, your successes, and your failures.

For the most part, your paradigms didn't originate with you. They're the accumulated inheritance of other people's habits, opinions, and belief systems. Yet they remain the guiding force in YOUR life.

Negative and faulty paradigms are why ninety-some percent of the population keeps getting the same results, year in and year out." - Bob Proctor

You'll be amazed at how being vulnerable, owning your story, and having the self-image to dream big will open doors. The people who come into your life are not by accident. They are there because you attracted them. The doors that open for you are not a coincidence; they open because you will then have the ability to see them. The negativity will come less frequently because you will learn to control whether you become emotionally involved. These things don't happen overnight, but I assure you, it absolutely does happen. Becoming aware of who you are, what you desire, and having the strength to let go of what doesn't support that is just the beginning of your joy. Allow yourself to feel joy. Find it in everything you see and do. You will find that what brings you joy will flow to you easily and without effort, as you are a magnet of what you think about most. Decide what you desire to be a magnet of.

The ending paragraphs of this chapter are part of the speech to my real estate office after I began the Bob Proctor coaching program. The office team leader asked me to talk about one thing that I'd attribute any business success to. Here is some of what I said to the room full of other agents:

"After much personal growth, the need for change, digging deep on what it is that I'm here for— my purpose—I've learned that what we need to be successful is not one more tool or the one-million-dollar idea that's going to get us to the top ... it's our paradigm. It's how we think. And this, my friends, is no easy thing to change. It takes a level of awareness. You can consciously know all the right things to do, but what stops you from doing them is your unconscious mind, your paradigm.

Most of what we believe is formed for us before we even are aware of it. It's no coincidence I have the same degree from the same university as my siblings. We all come from the same tree, so to speak.

So then why did I constantly feel like a lion in a cage? I didn't know why I felt that way at the time, but I knew I was frustrated and meant for more. I just didn't know what was stopping me from going after it.

So, I read. And I attended mostly everything I could as I knew I needed to grow. I had it all figured out, yet I was still feeling like I wasn't making progress on where I knew I wanted to be. Do you remember feeling alive? LIKE REALLY alive? What was it that made you feel that way? I believe that's not placed there by accident. I believe that's your purpose. And if we can't define what makes us feel alive, then we must be doing just the opposite ... slowly dying. Scary, isn't it? I'd say that's how most people live. We live to keep our family and friends happy, we listen to their advice (even if they don't have what we want), we become a product of our own environments, and we justify why we aren't completely fulfilled because that's 'just for other people' or 'it's selfish to want more than what I'm blessed with now.'

Is it selfish if you work for it? Is it selfish if it fulfills your purpose? What's selfish is NOT going after your passion. Living small is what's selfish. By not pursuing the talent you were born with, you are cheating the world by not doing what you were born to do. Our Creator did not, does not, and will not create us to be complacent or mediocre. Our Creator didn't handpick the 1% and say, 'You'll change the world, but these small people aren't meant for that.' NO! Our Creator made each of us unique. The ones who changed the world are the ones who went after it and made a difference. They are the ones who believed they could. They found their passion and let nothing else get in the way. You are unique!

If everything in life is abundant, isn't it crazy to think that abundant lives are only for other people? I am not speaking of abundance as in only wealth. An abundant life is joy in all areas. What makes those who we desire to live like so special? I'll answer that for you. They figured out that they are worth it. They figured out that they can have anything they want in this life ... they realized that for it to come to fruition that they must first see it in their minds, believe it's theirs already, and work to achieve it. Not work harder, not work more, but being focused on what they desire, and saying no to anything else that's not in line with it. I'm speaking professionally, physically, spiritually, etc.

I challenge you today to dig deep, ask yourself, what do you want? What makes you feel alive? What is it that sets your soul on fire? If you're not sure, go back to childhood. What did you dream about?

So with that said, here's my secret sauce. My biggest lesson: I now think about what my mom would say to me today. Here's the kicker ... She's with her Creator. She is free from the chains that were placed here on Earth. She is free from the paradigm she grew up with, and she is now 100% her true self. What would she say to me now? Would she tell me to break free from all the negative self-talk? Would she tell me to live fully? Would she tell me to make the difference that I know I'm put on this Earth to do? Would she tell me that anything is possible? I believe she would. I believe she wants me to fly. So, before you look for the secret sauce, or the one thing that will propel your business the fastest, I know, without a doubt, that that comes from within. When you ask yourself, 'How do I succeed?' first, know that you are worth it. Do what you love doing in your business. We are all unique, so what works for one person may not make you feel alive. Whatever you do, do it fiercely, and do it consistently. When you love what you do, you do it well.

Know this—when you fixate on finding your purpose, on what makes you feel alive, and you KNOW you're worth it, the answers come to you. Remember this—the destination is not what's most important, it's the journey! You don't need to know how to get there, you just need to look for the next best step. It's who you become in the journey. That's the sauce.

I'll leave you with this. Don't wait for your world to get rocked to decide to change. You deserve greatness, no matter how it is that you define that."

No Shift—No Story

In this book, I've shared the not so pretty parts of my life. And here's why: It's important to realize that without a shift or a change, there really is no story to tell. I could have told you that I still think of myself as an airhead, a failure at relationships, a broke and broken single mom, and completely shattered from the losses I've experienced.

What kind of story would that be? Boring! Exhausting! One where you would not have made it to the end.

We don't hear about when others are in the worst part of their lives when they are going through it; we hear about the story of how they've overcome those times. We all have the people in our lives who are naysayers and continuously want to tell us how bad their lives are. These are the same people who do not change and prefer to bitch and complain about their lives. These are the people I avoid. I've been there, and all my bitching and complaining did for me was keep me there. I know better now, but I did not know then. We do the best we know how to do with the knowledge we have at the time. Continue to seek the truth. Continue to listen to your inner spirit. And know that if there is no shift, no growth, and no change, there is no good story! Where in your life do you need to tell a different story? Make the shift. Make the change. Make it the best life experience you know how.

Allow your lioness to roar and break free!

ABOUT THE AUTHOR

Brooke Krebill is the Director of Coaching and Agent Productivity within her brokerage, a top-producing Realtor, and a proud mother of two. After over a decade of Brooke being on a self-improvement journey, she is now coaching and mentoring others in finding their own true greatness. Visit Brooke at BrookeKrebill.com or follow her on facebook.com/uncagedbybrookekrebill.